T0125360

BOOKS BY ANDREW JORON

POETRY

The Sound Mirror (Flood Editions, 2008)

Fathom (Black Square Editions, 2003)

The Removes (Hard Press, 1999)

Science Fiction (Pantograph Press, 1992)

Force Fields (Starmont House, 1987)

PROSE

The Cry at Zero: Selected Prose (Counterpath Press, 2007)

Neo-Surrealism; Or, The Sun at Night: Transformations of Surrealism in American Poetry, 1966-1999 (Black Square Editions, 2004; revised and expanded ed. Kolourmeim Press, 2010)

COLLABORATIONS

Force Fields with Brian Lucas (Hooke Press, 2010)

Invisible Machines with Robert Frazier and Thomas Wiloch (Jazz Police Books, 1993)

TRANSLATIONS

The Footsteps of One Who Has Not Stepped Forth by Richard Anders (Black Square Editions, 2000)

Literary Essays by Ernst Bloch (Stanford University Press, 1998)

TRANCE ARCHIVE

CITY LIGHTS SPOTLIGHT SERIES NO. 3

ANDREW JORON

TRANCE

ARCHIVE

NEW

AND

SELECTED

POEMS

CITY LIGHTS

SAN FRANCISCO

Poems from *The Sound Mirror*. Copyright © 2008 by Andrew Joron.
Reprinted with the permission of Flood Editions.

CITY LIGHTS SPOTLIGHT
The City Lights Spotlight Series was founded in 2009, and is
edited by Garrett Caples, with the assistance of Maia Ipp.

Library of Congress Cataloging-in-Publication Data
Joron, Andrew.
Trance archive : new and selected poems / by Andrew Joron.
p. cm. – (City lights spotlight ; no. 3)
ISBN 978-0-87286-530-3
1. Science fiction poetry, American. 2. Fantasy poetry, American.
3. Experimental poetry, American. I. Title. II. Series.
PS3560.O766T73 2010
811'.54–dc22
2009042025

Cover image © Brian Lucas, *Possible* (detail)
http://notabove-notbelow.blogspot.com

All City Lights Books are distributed to the trade by
Consortium Book Sales and Distribution: www.cbsd.com

For small press poetry titles by this author and others,
visit Small Press Distribution: www.spdbooks.com

City Lights Books are published at the City Lights Bookstore,
261 Columbus Avenue, San Francisco, CA 94133

www.citylights.com

CONTENTS

For one
Rose
    out of Reason

ABSOLUTE BLACK CONTINUUM

A

bout before: A forced first defines difference.

B

one.

C

saw.

D

light.

E

merge, mere germ.

F

face final line.

G

ode, crystal-encrusted, stressed structure to chime.

H

    to woe, each to woo: the water of thought.

I

    am, wham wham, who am. Hide head.

J

    bird: A word whirred, bared.

K

    bull charged & buried. List as lost, chill billions: pent rage,
    repent.

L

    a mental metal. Untooled, untold.

M

    pinnacled upon a whirlwind: a voice-vehicle, a vastest test of
    heaven.

N

    o.

O

   pen.

P

   eel, free from form, writing writhing.

Q

   bed, the bound of sound, sole solid of air.

R

   eyes arise. Our hour essay.

S

   say our hour.

T

   eat of the mean of, the meat of, matter & mother.

U

   too are two.

V

   ear, revere.

W

double me, melodious labor.

X

isle of beauty. A soiled boot. A boat that sails into the sun.

Y

knot untied, united in the not attained.

Z

row of zeroes, row of roses & of rows.

UNTILED

Or, outside the mosaic law.

In leaf, relief
That that pattern never repeats.
      Saturn, turn as
Alpha laugh, omega game.

The biggest signal
Begins against
      gain

For foreign rain—
For
      a man, amen.

Jazz is the edge of every age, the
Lair of all alarm.

Static, the

State

States

    O there, other—

    a sentence given to the forgiven.

MONAD, NOMAD

1.

He resided in the mind of winter.

I said, "He resided in the mind of winter."

I heard you: you sighed, "I said, 'Sad eye, essayed.'"

Who, as history's stars, steers stares, & stairs, & stores?

I said, sad eye, "I desire as I design."

To call tall column, you you you you you molecule.

'Til *tell* fell fatal—

As cold is coiled upon a recessive center, or eye of poverty.

2.

Changeless change, a signature of things that sings.

Thus, the plural is applied to a singular glow.

3.

Mind, signed rind.

A a body, boding dying.

Imagination ash, then engine.

Up, flee, leaf. Wind up wind.

To the vent, the event.

O coeval with without. Add shadow: *vocation.*

SKYMAP UNDER SKIN

Ache, a network
Is & is
     a naked
Entirety, a knotted Not.

Bluest semblance of
     myself, the aleph
Unblessed.

Announce
Anything, the name is mine—
     a tear, a ware.

A
     substance
     stood under
The sob at the base of the body.

       To render random

Saying
       sewing

A wing on air.

On errancy's errand—

Vague wave over day, given
       some
       same

Name, my nightdark mark, my mouth without—

EARTHWARD

Where in the actless occult air to
Share sheer shore?

Enunciate solace, less sun.
Main
        name, refer to refire.

Revise *eyes* over
        sees, wave-woven.

The same, the semen, the
        parody of paradise.

        O hoarded dead—

Old word *hark*, old word *dark*—
Old word
        old, old world.

A BEAUTIFUL DISEASE

After he lay in a soft room/diffuse with ices
That was called the Cube of Day

& looked at clouds that passed
His window—an upside-down
Accelerated landscape
. . . a mirror for the collapse
Of mountains

In Kepler's head
The outer planets played
Disquieting harmonies of the dead

Other, video-engendered
Friends would whisper to him, read & decay
In spiral-calculations

But half a man is tired of these voices
That drip lost numbers
Beneath a drone of fishpipes; or leak

An ocean's Moon-drawn
Phrase—dense as vital juices run
From severed objects around his bedside

nature morte
One votive jar of poison bees
A steel etching
Nerve-portrait of his future body

Stained instruments, that force
Food & water upward
To the surface of this amniotic sphere

triomphe du rêve
Out of the wall there grow
Long sensitive tongues
Administering to his childhood—pale
Servants, forever silenced—gray newsreels
Of a parallel past, that show invading armies

& pinned to the door
A viral snowflake

The mind snared
      in its diamond saliva
As nurses trace, with
Well-trained fingers
Cold & faintly shining . . . open valves

A street of roofless
Empty houses
Where he saw the Contaminated
Ships set sail
& women, undressed of their flesh
Fly away
In the dreams of wild animals

EVENT HORIZON

As life is alien to the Earth, so language is alien to life. Between
them, there can be no resemblance: each one is the mortal remains of
the other. It is a work of dissolution to ascend from the order of the
Rock to that of the Eye to the Idea. At one level are the motiveless
atoms, the worlds their sediment, light itself in constant darkening
(aftereffect of the spontaneous collapse of a singularity). At a higher
level, communication also is a process of decay: the breaking-apart
of an incommunicable Unity. Life—in relation to the vastness of
the energy flux in language—is wasteland, preserving a stasis in all
its teeming that is equal to the silence of the pre-biotic Earth. Every
event is the opening of a new abyss.*

---

* These are the decipherments of runes found on the shielding of various "Relativ-
istic Sepulchers" that have lately begun to materialize on the fused plain at Izmir.

MIRROR OF PROMETHEUS

The vial is shattered, his head
Encircled
By the birds of disaster

A stain like diseased light
      follows his every movement
A solar seepage
In human shape—the relic
Of his brain
Installed
As a radio inside a broken statue

He listens
On the forbidden channel: a New Order
Is pronounced

Time-shards contain him
Secretly
In their just proportion

In gems, disposed at random
Over bare earth

All their compass
Would be a chorus measure
Of the degrees his spine can bend

The iron prongs of his ribs
Creak open like antique gates

       organ of life
       grinding on
In grand sustain under a starless dome

The gravities
Of unseen presences distort the past
       a dull & steady rhythm
In his ear / are prayers to immense machinery
Underground

& his skin is made
To flow away—another landscape of flower-animals
Whose helio-plasms

Show an architecture
      similar to Plato's *Laws*
Dawn-whitened porticos
Redolent with nepenthe & musk
The judgment of the gods
Again is issued: a floating rhomboid
The knife rises
The skies boding information silence

Rituals of the world's end become
Randomized as Paradise
In a window in the air
(eternal friend of fire)—he watches
The obsolete biomasses
Of Europe, Africa & Asia
      returning home
—gently spin in freefall

The mineral Idea
Evolves toward senescence; & he waits
      the light scraping at his eye

His screams are phonemes
In a language about to be invented

POST-HISTORIC PASTORALE 2

At the end of every avenue
In the circular city
There stares a monumental Eye of Power
     empinnacled
     on a whirlwind

Inaudibly it roars . . . subliminal commands
& blessings hourly

Under the eye: grain molders in silos
The weather is changed into an ideogram
     that is not for us
     to understand

I AM JOE'S BRAIN

What are my simulacra saying to me this morning?
    the bright broken bodies
Are hung
All over the walls of my room
They are saying: "Go out and earn a living
Then come home and kill us once again!"

I go out into the stacked cubicles of the world-city
Work is an endless pounding of pistons
    a reading of screens
        covered with pink and green revolving toroids
Info-mosaics
That deliver me
Squared images of Jesus
Quitting time: I put on my rubberoid leisure-mask
Muscle into the standing masses
    of commuters on the slideway

S*T*Y*L*E today is: everyone walks
    with the herky-jerky gait of silent movie ancestors

O the radio tower reminds me
      of the skeleton of my lady
With her halo of jagged dark lightning

Of the word *inviolate*
O the voluble, the volatile sound

AUBADE: TAU CETI

A transparent pyramid sings
To greet the morning
We flow & shudder in our dream pools
Spiky tendrils
Wound tight around communication-coils

Our latest theorem
Presses Time into thin blue rectangles
That we who rise mirror-like
Out of the nimbus of sound
May repair those silent interfaces

A memory-system / uncontrolled
Spreads in fractures
Across the sea of quartz
—eye-tips spark on
Brittle awakening

Let voice seed in our vacancy
& hymn to Antithesis, O star-inseminated
Series. . . Brood of echoes

Sediment of ancestors
That hardens to clearest stone / here
Let us dwell in hollow cells
Of a night-abandoned body

Glazed with reason. Our dialogue
Tunnels the Maternal mound

As quelled populations
Choir into sentience; overswarm
Her cathedral-carcass

The sky-lobes
Trade in Her electricities
The reborn / reburn

THE INVENTION OF ZERO

The mind, a freezing reptile
Sits exposed upon a ledge
     space falls away
     in all directions

There is no sky
Enclosing this new world
     the wind's last breath
Returns into the cave

The shields
     of a post-historic army
Uncoil like minor suns

     a hierarchy of bells
Cascades to a silent equilibrium

—second skin
Of an escapeless circle

Its reflection
Expansive as a sea-surface
　　　flattened
　　　by the weight of the invisible

CONFESSIONAL

Where the spires of the mirror-Prague
Point downward to the Earth's core

I have watched *pneuma*, spirit-pale
Pour out of the ear
      of a sleeping man

That man was I, carcerated
In a crystal of medieval Winter

I have lain in reverse agony
      along the fracture-plains
Of the calm & necessary voice

Perfect
      & future tenses
Lend their cloud-perspectives
To my insistent dying

My Old High German
Verbs, all shadow-measures
        dictated from afar
Mount as evidence
In hidebound ledgers

So I allow: this tusk of ebony
Surrounded by white roses
        is aerial
            to forbidden Musick

This ceiling
        of sweating stone
Fits into the architecture
Of a universal puzzle

I have heard such iron
Tongue-told sufferings

Tabulate the moral constants
The wooden wheels
        that stop & turn

AUTOPLASTIK

The orbiting reflector
Turns night into day: petals *ping*

Accelerated workers
    swarm into the plaza
A blur on the soul's dead instrument

Everywhere, windows are blanked
To the same newsreel

I alone
Inhabit a mockup of the early nineteenth century

I, the great idealist
    who confesses
On the first page of his diary: *Father!*
There are no living atoms

& the diary answers: *Identity*
Is that
Which is eaten from within

Another man is partially assembled
On the table

Another module
Unshrouded, revolves in sunlight

      filtered through noise
A simulated victory

Crawls like a glove
Animated by music

CONFESSION: ON METHOD

1.

I longed for the discovery of sound. My surroundings were evolving slowly toward recognition — no walls or people existed as yet, only their categories: the embryos of birds, the unopened eye of a window.

I had practiced the art of swooning — of allowing one's perceptions, previously exact and parallel as the folds of a curtain —

Swirl of coordinates, like the hem of a gown, to be gathered up, so as not to brush against — I was allowed to fall backward, into the arms of — But there is no word, no *sound*, to serve as object here.

My cry, withheld, was described by the arc that shone dimly — the limb of a letter, or starry Cross near the invention of writing.

Logos was a ghost, or mirror that held the whirlpool-image of its origin — so it was given to me, Word incarnate, compound of delirium, dissolving on my tongue —

A cistern, or sky, where sight was poured. Space was overloaded with aspects of vanishing: *Melancholia*, my visible mind, was shamed by its innocence in the face of obscurity.

Hooded, I had premeditated Time, a lesson in self-division.

There was divine mockery of my weakness, my fable about a spire of flesh; and the names that "blood sang."

What consonants answered the mystery of the vowels, in a chorus rising toward the bodiless? I lay disheveled, exposed beneath a dome.

Whatever I was, was written. Close to — closing to — a moment that was proximate, impervious, and final.

2.

    archaic torso : in shadow-rotation

    equivalence, a burden : lost optic

    a moving center : the Earth made weightless

the hidden : folds within simplicity

calculus, for what calling : between the veils

intervals, the Unanswering : exfoliant

of rending : of rendering

tears, through tears : gauze over gaze

terminus over term : Surrender

sunless, whose peaks : who speaks

solace : words given up to

no other, fused : refused

3.

Telling the Silences, incendiary within every code.

— flight of the Alone to the Alone.

— attempted signature, leaking into structure: the hand memorious of the fires of its making.

Of logic, the unfastenings, joined at the vertex of all possible statements.

Of space & its responses, the endless recess. Realism that underlies the name, buried in its own transparency.

— coils everlasting through sensation's hollows, a shell of concentric hells.

Preliminary to blindness, revision. Form is given by that which it cannot contain.

— a blank page is the flag of a secret conflagration.

Turned inside out, so that flesh enspheres a central star.

Birthplace of the first displacement.

System of systems, where an Inhuman mechanism is learning to weep. Being absolutely porous, to absorb the mortal body.

Sites of abandonment stand for the letter A.

Asylum's analytic, accumulating zeroes, antinomies, atoms.

Unheard dissonance, whose harmonic arcs — curling across the Original void — fall sideways into lines of script.

—"after the end, before the beginning." Law that weighs its own likenesses, the ways of its release—

LE NOMBRE DES OMBRES

The faster I travel
    the slower the world dies

Inside the head of a flower
The sun's
    a swinging pendulum

—all Radiance is progress
Of a pre-existent stillness

Stone, inspired
To fluency

    curves thought
    toward the drinking of Its shadow

  grail: grille: grid

The lines recursive to impalement

one point alone
      sings cumulative, crowding negativity

My apparitions
      distorted by star-tides
Fail to approximate zero

Where sensation's tip
Crumbles to ash

Another
Radio-profile turns, edged with dark cries

      objects unfounded
      of medieval prophecy
The heavens too grow cold

A HOLE IN TRANSLATION

1.

If there is a *floor*
It is a *flare*
      too quick & too bright
      to be trod upon.

Enter *here*
Inter *here*
      —turn among
      the torn, the Entire.

      —a lexicon seems mysterious
Because it is inhabited by no one.

(Sense alone
Has many senses.)

To remember is to sew the body
      back together. To forget

Is to scatter, to sow.

To read life backwards, then
To walk upon the Moon.

"I have learned the ABC of pure contigency. Now I follow words
as these follow one another: footprints over frozen ground."

    as if
A primary
      aimless-
        ness were fixed within Sequence.

The line, diverted into itself.
    (One object
Before the first & after the last.)

The voice, a relic of writing.
Rows of integers extending beyond the rose.

2.

As if the totality of all possible statements
        formed but a single statement.
A self-refuting one.

A text, or only its stranded
        title, pointing to
        an anti-text beyond all possibility.

It is a title that initiates a series of fissures leading to the ruin of the
work. The capital words, literally words "at the head," are also
decapitated ones, the first to be exiled or estranged from the body of
the text.

And what becomes of the interval, the forsaken sky, *between* the
title and the rest? Perhaps it is a rehearsal for erasure—a timeless
horizon reflected in the oceanic instability of all the terms that are
spread beneath it. . .

This argument has been grown from a crystal of salt.

—translating the Inhuman: "Robbed of its prayer-cry, an incomplete thought will shatter into droplets of electricity."

Mere copies of copies, worlds upon worlds: a language's rotting intertext. A plagiarism, versed in these slowly ripening accords—

3.

The bodiless
Enters through the ears & nostrils.

Incense, & the blackening
     of parallels upon convergence.

The first
     word: *red*
     string against string.
The second:
Fluted through a hollow bone.

That the exponent
Of the skin = space.

That each word = an aerial fastness
Previous to the mind.

That awakening = the coincidence of
Waves without locality:

       sense as sense
       sense as sound
       sound as sound.

       "aus dem tonlosen Los"

       —a curving wall, a well.

Crescent ((of culmination) of exclusion).
Of ((of) of)

4.

In isolation.
That speaking = falling backward into one's own body.

In constellation.
That listening = becoming bodiless.

Thus, the idea of a horn that has been emptied of music.
An emptiness of many chambers.

> "That ship
> is stranded among the Horse Heaven Hills."

As landscape advances its mute iterations: small accidents accumulate, cloud-like, into the shapes of history.

Bird-like, the silhouette of the castle.

(Dawn breaks at the moment when night withdraws, undiminished, into consciousness.)

—once spilled, their senses were drunk by the dust. The message (that the object is missing) is both involuted and involuntary.

More unwritten characters: crowned by white coronas. Meaning as "total eclipse." Nudity's raiment, shifting in response to a color more elemental than mirror.

If A, then not *not* A = warring states flank the sign of equivalence.

The house that stood still.

SERIALISM, RECONSIDERED

1. The Daughter's Decomposing Music

What seas seize, sees
What conclusions race
    toward, may
    erase their distant Motives

What stops, spots
    dusk, sun-sung between

Chance & structure
Her gender is Botany

    her knowledge, the color of Water

To truly perceive
Is to be reborn. The wild answer

Is no answer, communicant

without issue, her source or

sorcery, nerves strung

Harp-like

To the tinctures of evening

as if joy were

Vestigial of stone, concealing cold

allusive

Touch, elusive, illusive touch—harmonic

Threads

thrown down

where the hands

Recollect their shadows, empty pyramids

once-solar

Thoughts. Unheard-of, passing "slower

Than time." So echoic

come her strokes—which

Must guard against, while
    building, the inaudible magnitudes

2. The Modifications

Epistemologies of fire had blackened the page ("elements" had
been changed to "ailments," "the soul" to "the soil").

That "statutes" father "statues"— common ancestor of Night and
the picture that never left his eyes. According to the Gnostics, giv-
ing birth is tantamount to causing a death.

According to the alphabet, "lost" follows "last"—the witness was
a gaping hole, a good book. The body of a man is buried inside the
laws of motion.

Refrain, refrain. "Exfoliant": emerging out of madness.

He wrote: "I, the messenger of Reason, was instructed to contact
the agent, or the angel, of Despair." Where? asked the voiceless
voice. "In Samarkand, among the subterranean levels of Ulugh
Beg's observatory."

—numbers sorted through the sieve of a new Millennium: the populace below, streaming through the city gates. Fearful of the comet—but a true story is devoid of both characters and events.

He read the sentence over again, watching the mechanical keys move of their own accord. He was a worker, a shadow-carver, not a philosopher making love to his own death.

—an emptiness "riddled" by atoms. (Reflexive dust, ashes: have they always assumed the shape of this question?)

Space itself, a roomful of whispers.—He blew softly into the resemblances: the openings.

3. The Unwhole: The Unhealing

—ruined edge of knowledge

Orison
Horizon. The "bleeding blade"

of the hypotenuse

As if a perfect line were capable of imbalance: disbelief of night's verge
upon a verge in Light.

A number that cannot be
Folded against or *into* itself

"Der Untergang des Abendlandes"
        as taught by Pythagoras

A paradoxical shadow
Pointed *towards* the Sun

A literal star impaled at the imaginary center. An unlikely pattern of
redundancy within a signal of pure noise. . .

TORN SPACE AROUND POE

[. . .]

What a desperate trance!—The skyboat resembles a flying vulva; the city, the arc of an abandoned soliloquy.

Writing is disguised as perception's ghost, a nocturnal substance to be spread by the Sun. In the future, flames will possess the stillness of objects stolen from the past.

Accuracy is hopeless if unintentional. now demonstrates the mirror's pull, its perfume: everything has (always, already) suffered countless iterations.

Eyes: the emblems of the invisible. Hands: the instruments of renunciation. Head a crumbling turret that at evening collects such thoughts like crows—

There exists a set of objects made up of those objects that do not belong to any set.

There exists an uncorrupted Text: a Boat built out of the sliding surfaces of the sea.

THE HERETIC OF RAVENS

     "if
One existed, it would immediately become Two.
Therefore

One is not innocent, & the Infinite
       (because Divine) must be less than One."

Under the green sky—
The purple flesh of this impossible fruit.

       All-too-human
       fact or factor, its limbs askew

Whose fear is my
Multiple. Inhabiting a sphere, forever

       open-mouthed, outshining light—

My labors, bird-encircled.
Collecting words

Then linking them in phrases
Expulsed from Eden

      & voiceless as waves
      repeating axioms of accidental harmony.

Hung upside down
      where the state's lotteries
Administer to the poor.

Unto them I say: "Renounce your birthdays!
The sun is a variable star!"

Society in its nakedness—a cubism
Of cells within cells.

Awaiting the advent of—
      a tower, a tunnel.
No
      difference between *immanence* & *imminence*.

Creation has no door.

PECULIAR ROOTS HAVE REASON'S EYES

As mineral is changeful
Within the fixity of its lament

Rays raise Earth
To a semblance of waves, to
       words out of order

      the data invoked
By a dying choir—*There is rage*
     in the body's sequences

Neither sense, nor object
But an unfinished ratio

Heard as a curve
      continuous with endings
As a vowel is laden

With air's ores, the sky subterranean
To that skin

let weather accelerate
Below the horizon, circumference of
        a bell. Sound, divided

From sound, ancient
In its approaches—the rung silences

To be spoken. Any name, to fructify
As the famine of its presence

        —lightning's most intricate delay

THE FAST SECRET

Tooled finely. Told finally.

Through the spy-hole one glimpses a coelenterate floating in mid-air, impossible allegory of the genitals.

Who inspects a blank spot? No one today can read the artifice of nature.

Glossing the limbs of the nude—

Star, *scar*, words burnt to Conclusion—A radiant plan, as of streets convergent, vanishes in perspective, where the Predicate of Beauty offers only violence without body—this moment, the knife-point itself, being Indivisible.

By a cunning stratagem, all of the words are recirculated as whorls within another medium, resistant as glass.

The spell of rhetoric, the spill of—

Signatures pouring through gaps in the blood.

Pure Witness—Mirrored vertex (laborer's sweat). Thesis of knife against knife, the Embrace of necessity.

Some additional paragraphs from Marx, quoting Burckhardt on ancient cities.

The scene is lit oddly, as if from below.

Among the toppled columns, little Theater of the Hunt, the men are waiting to kill a stag. To rebuild its head, as Human shadow—

—its sinews strung to perfect ratios.

In this place, whose skin, skewed to plus or minus—

Aversive pleasure in the contemplation of—

A line tangential to every point in space (the lost wager), expressed as a random scrawl. A modus for inscribing *destiny* upon *density*, *solid* upon *soiled*.

A mood, extravagant, that underlies the governance of matter. Its processionals gone, piping and whirling to nothing.

First words: all that has collected in the traps of silence.

To be doubled, bled between two horizons. Economy of the poles of Night, where the pictures are exchanged.

Face of the Sun inside a mirror, to serve as a weapon—

—when certain "useless" glands (long ignored by philosophers), embedded in our brains like eyes turned inward, like sleeping wasps, will awaken at last, to sting us with new Perceptions, & leave us stumbling, in a state of "dispassionate bewilderment"—

In early childhood, object relations are reversed, or have steepened to ice-lattices. So that a ball sobs for its nearness to a bell—

—riff that falls down deeper than rhythm, defeating the final cause—

Blue diagrams of a world without gravity.

Clouds, letters, broken shapes of breath.

To subtract the sea from its numberless waves is a contribution of the mind.

FROM "FATHOM"

1.

Climb to climate, the awe of O's
Fiery circumference.

Not to justify this (spillage of integers).
Not to be eaten but spoken (as a "seed" or a "seeming").

Muscular skill, the red-rippling
Curtains, the deep interior of the play.

The motions all unrehearsed
Lunar risings, slow crescendos, cries against God—

    a self-refuting silence.

Commentary

The finest jest is made "in advance of" the jester.

A new generation of snails, with "eyes that are horns of the moon"—

"The Propositions," *The Distances*.

Here a plagiarist assumes the place of the author.

2.

Earth rose
In a gown of white air

On the morning of an endless night.
Soundless as the Book

—a bone Garden of artificial sound.
The desert's listening instrument—

At this game of decay's cadences
You win your second skin.

An empty repetition initiates the series.

—ciphers, sapphires. *Veers* round & round *reveres*.

Reading is an act of intervention that remains blank—whose im-
mobility (re)joins writing at the very moment of its (always unreal-
ized) origin.

Writing's blood is invisible but meant to be red.

A memory of the Not-Yet (abandoned city). At its center, there
stands a misshapen statue of living minerals, neither natural nor
artificial. Everywhere the light aims at a vanishing point: now is the
late hour of the commentary.

3.

What fateful door hinges
On the difference between "shall" & "will"?

All *shall* vanish into their futurity.
None *will* question their intent.

The face of the Other who refuses to wake
Resembles a clock.

That entry was lost, that was the entrance
To this Time of writing —

    where the eyes of effacement were hoarded.

Commentary

If, in reading, we "invite the shadow," we press a word to reveal its lost priority—

Such tension has its characteristic color: a star striated throughout the folds of flesh.

Here, the subject is allowed to walk backward into the mirror of subjection.

Here, the decanted words flow back into the vessel's mouth.

FROM "CONSTELLATIONS FOR THEREMIN"

with birds in his hair he goes forth —Celan

Your flesh of rose – your hair of birds —Goll

That birds become points or musical notes; & that hair, horizontal lines or staves. . .

Hands are entangled in a force field to make music.
Hands are birds caught in the hair of the theremin.

"The closer I approach you, the more you sink into the abyss of pre-existant objects."

"In vain you paint hearts on the window: a god goes among the hordes."

Note: The epigraphs are my translations, from the German, of the lines at issue in the Paul Celan/Yvan Goll plagiarism controversy. The lines occur in, respectively, Celan's book of poems *Poppy and Remembrance* (1952) and Goll's book *Dream-herb* (1951). Passages given in quotes but left unattributed are also translated from these books.—AJ

Flights of birds tune the strings of a destroyed or not-yet-invented instrument.

Pictures of ancient noise, hieratic news. Suggesting hair, birds, & the blue banners of the invisible.

A necklace of hands —Celan

A necklace of larksongs —Goll

The first book holds the letters of the last. Never to be corrected or corrupted, but thrown into the mouth of earth.

Memory is reduced to monument; unseen weight that bends the poppy, a perennial herb with milky juice, also known as the dreaming herb.

"We walk toward the single great eye that hangs over clouds in the forehead of a sullen thinker."

"Shells do I utter and thin clouds, and a hull sprouts in the rain. . . Black the portal springs open, I sing."

Fate foretold in tallow light: "silent circling lamps" lend a deeper hue to the jar of wasps, the bottle of air.

Voice, never-arriving wave. The sound of the theremin sorrows over the absolute whiteness of the sick man's blood.

In the form of a wild boar
your dream stamps through the woods at evening's edge. —Celan

The wild boars with magical triangular heads
They stamp through my decaying dreams —Goll

Magic cannot be seen or named. Better to banish the word, or show how black sublates white: as the German *rein*, the French *rien*.

Consider the line, with its mutually exclusive endpoints. To be exiled is the true homecoming. What, then, is the nature of self-evidence?

"And you and I with starry crowns: Proof eternal against the doom of time."

"So that a ripening like yours will enrapture the festive Eye that has wept such stones."

In this tale of the body, errors accumulate without fail. Victory tomorrow will be measured by the sun's refusal to rise.

Slavery will end, as the peripatetic argued, when the Loom weaves without a hand to guide it, or when the Lyre plays itself.

The suns of death are white —Celan

a sacred dagger slashes our death-sun —Goll

The crisis of the object creates an image without analogy. From reference to face to face: *between* will bind its twin, or twist detail to overarching feature.

Such words must turn inside out in order to stay the same.

"The cry, the human cry out of the lightless body that like a sacred dagger slashes our death-sun." Solar cry that according to Copernicus inhabits the center of every voice.

"The suns of death are white like the hair of our child, who climbs out of the flood as you pitch a tent upon the dunes. Our child, who brandishes the knife of happiness over us with extinguished eyes."

Mergence of crime & cry in "the crisis of the object." An emergency everlasting. Hands shy away from this immaculate damage; the same hands hover over the throat of the theremin.

Scratched-out script: bloodline of unstable constellations.

TRANCE ARCHIVE

"No" goes
Where the war of analogy allows—
"Stop" to start, "house" to walk roofless & aflame.

In *Principia*, the solid of least resistance
      is language—Moon
More earthlike than the Earth.

      Prose is the ocean of that shore—
      that, unauthored, revises & erases
      its propositions.

New entry under "singing" or "singeing"—
      lines closed or disclosed
      under accelerating clouds.

Only the fingertips of the eyes
Can touch this distance.
      It is a kind of cold fire.

What surplus is hidden
In the place of in the place of?
        Mirror, to remain unmoved, divides its answer.

So light itself, thrown into fact, opposes
        everything revealed.
Unravelled thread: the letter's perfect Form.

As talk opaques the breath—
Tenebrae aches in the mark of the marrow.
The plural to violate the verb, verbless to bless.

        Troubled, bled traceries in series
        as the downed sound dawned.
All's aligned, annulled, annealed, axioms

        made anxious in imitation of vanishing.
Accidental universal—
The imperative to pour, poor, pure, to no purpose.

Again an agony of

like paired with like, skin
pared from fruit, no

Vaster than its voiceprint, standing still
To escape itself
      instead of dancing like a skeleton.

Echo
      that precedes the call, the premise.
White moth, whiter mother—

"No" goes to no beginning. The audience of the dead
      gathers at this barrier, this
      deafening defining—

      No, volume
      whose head is cleaved, that leaks an inkling
      of last things.

"No" goes to "noise" then to "ghost."
To separate corrupted curtains, to open the book
      behind the book—

SPINE TO SPIN, SPOKE TO SPEAK

The pilot alone knows
That the plot is missing its
Eye.

Why isn't this "ominous science"
        itself afraid, a frayed
Identity?

Pray, protagonist—
Prey to this series of staggered instants.

Here the optic
Paints its hole, its self-consuming moment.
It is speech, dispelled, that
        begs to begin to ache.

So that *wind* accelerates to *wound*, a dead sound
        enlivened by the visitation of owls.

As pallid as parallel, the cry
Of the negative is not the negative
     of the cry—an irreparable blessing—

A green world's
     "sibilant shadows" where
The syllables of your name are growing younger.

As involuntary as involuted, "who"
     returns its noun
     to each tender branch
That *noon* breaks into *no one*.

Point of view
Hovers, a circular cloud, over evacuated
Time.

That heard its herd bellow below
     the terraced cities, the milled millions

     as sold as unsouled, ghost-cargos.

A symptom of the Maddening—
Woman undressed of her flesh.
Man's address
      to Thou, & the flag of Thou.

How the fallen state
Meets the starry horizon, veil
   against witness, hunger against void.

O, oldest
      outermost Other—

Ageing mask
Of the transparent Earth. Unspeculated
      image
Streaked with mirror & stricken words.

You are neither the torn, nor the thorn.

You are the many-petalled
      melting point of repeating decimals. . .

Receiver, river
Has been burned into voice, a day-dark ribbon.

All signal is this
Single.

MAZED INTERIOR

1.

Cogs & cogs that cannot turn
     to recognitions: such dogs in the dark noonday!

As if the tongue told & tolled
Among
     the melancholic arcades.

Where the *moods* advance toward the *modes*.

Time to try the knot, the Not
Or to be caught
Forever in nerve-traceries of Beauty. . .

Unstrung, the structure is sound.

2.

Detour to far fires.

To be counted missing. . . in a toroidal space
That mimics the shape of its container, speech.

The passive of, the possessive of—

Measureless intent, *blue* almost *black*, the picture
        below the voice.
Less a name than a substance

Coming to stillness, star-inhabited.
Less a substance than a sigh.

3.

Awaited, thou, *unawaited*. Divided here. O

then
Opened as earthen
        ring, cave-recorded.

A mazed interior. Self-similar aisles of isles, pouring
        form from form.

Lastness as device. Aligned as measurements (letters) —

        as sensitive, all-too-sensitive compass
        needles forever seeking
        the frozen pole, the zero.

Caption: "An end-of-century sailing ship, *Delirium*
        held fast in sheets of ice."

4.

No atmosphere is sufficient.

An embryo in the brain is not yet breathing.

There, the labor
Of the living rock, where an ache, or bruise-ember
      will be discovered.

Scored
      for Theremin, or permanently scarred.

Where shadows point: *Mad* lengthening to *made*, as unmade
      scaffolding.

      Thus, repetition, resisted
      is the register of thought.
Now here, even as staves are falling, another story

—intervallic—cannot be told—that is, besieged

As the heart encaged in bone.

The animal calls *long long*, disconsolate
In its hollow mountain.

5.

Neither nor nor neither, time builds
Its twelve tones between *round* & *ruined*.

—as the roots of the sunflower, arrayed over earthlight.

Routes unreturning / term without terminus. Riding as reading
Migrates
        underground.

Writing as the righting
Of fallen
        angles, of tangles of Accident—

        arrives riven, a body never to be / surveyed.

Abandoned in a wintry field, the sum of its travels

—its hunting the same as its haunting.

DOLPHY AT DELPHI

FOR GARRETT CAPLES

No lesson but a lessening, a loosening.
The spiral is made to spill its center.

—a name that acts—imperative's axe
Loses its head

As a baritone (the low
        solo's slow slope) sax (imaginary
        gender needs no sleep).

How the wrong notes compose their own song

Parallel to a dream of drowned cities.

After hours, what style of address, what robes
        (robs us
Of daylight) of delight?

Tells, then shows
The *revel* hidden in *reveal*?

    —now's even later than the future. Found
    sound reduced to meaning.

The perpetual emotion of a star-like story.

WHAT SPILLS SPELLS

1. The Spoils

Neither raven nor haven, but a sound-drowned line.

All hollowed, no name is news to a drum.

The complete sentence holds its antlers high, antennae tuned to distant static.

Here a cloud is seeking a crowd, a clown a crown.

As "we," apparently ageless, converge upon a place of no resistance. Many words remain missing.

Now one of them—"rose"—appears to raise the dead. To the stillness inside the story.

Whose mouth—exponent of zero—repeats this order, aping the natural mask whose picture nominates speech.

To *hold* what is *holed*: reason's trapezoidal portrait.

The twin of (the body of) *between*.

In other words: appearance is a blind spot, a space of turbulence caused by an actor walking into a mirror—

Is, then, a "shine of recession" always to be posed against the interrogative? Perhaps.

2. The Spools

"Vanishing into visibility" is considered circus-like today.

Believer, return to the first erasure.

Resurrected for a hooded audience, a bird-winged book.

How a phrase freezes when sun-struck. To be illustrated by mourning, morning, and the abstractions induced by winter.

Doubt fills the margin of the page (confession of nudity).

Face averted, lacking every commentary. Soiled evidence, in ceaseless arrival—

Either "there is no time" or "there is no time."

How the mystical tenet *turns faster than* the groan of regret. This, within the same wheel of words.

Writing as the art of reading as rewriting.

"Drink me," says the dramatic sky. But there is no school for red weather, and the Moon shines with a borrowed light.

The hidden handprint is always represented.

3. The Spalls

So goes the *via negativa*. After the likeness of—

A riverbed (a porous science).

Alluvial fan opening meaning. Defined by, defied by, deified by, one word deposited upon another. Neither source nor mouth, but a crossed-out sacrifice.

How "the myth" is deposited upon "the mouth"—

Uncollected images of—

A rock's reckless reckoning. After magic, contingency itself appoints the letter A.

THE EVENING OF CHANCES

The leveling of chants is——

The etching of, the evening of, irregular glows. The various chases.
The chastening glove.

Pay attention: *the of is*, space, experience, emptiness.

No, slower than silence. Reward to reword, word-whirled world.

Frameless, the real is what we cannot look away from.

Every cause is an accident: so blue, trembling, awaits its turn.

Against begins, nudity without body.

Blue sister, who shows us how to disturb her rest. Revealed in the
grain: this deviance grown absolute.

Sheets of motion——writing——the blade that bleeds.

As the senses multiply, we look away to contemplate.

As the rains relate to ruins, as the bells——As the bells, bells, bells, bells, bells, bells, bells—

Can sameness answer its own secret? Here, the rains relate to ruins, & a dead tree has walked across the desert.

Such pauses repeat, but never return. Structure stretches into content, as trace over trance.

Let X represent the human cipher in a pose of astonishment. The future past is understood: we will have existed.

Understood here means *unsheltered*: not stood under. Similar to a prayer's elongated figure.

Cold noise collects in the listening devices. All blues & sciences.

THE MIRROR SOUND

Penned *A*
Cage confined
To page—

Lit, upon unlit lot, the
Letter
    O

—wrong sun, rung reason of

      One, that avatar of two. To
      One, who won't won't want—

      Here
O is I's

      avowal, a dead deed.
A gain to negate no gate.

So just my jest, my
Vote to *mon oeuvre*:

        vroom over room & verity, the

Straight arriving
        late to
Strayed, a raid upon the rayed.

I AM THE DOOR

I, my
      being to begin, my die
To decide my deicide, am

Gone again to distance, & sand, & stand

      by fear
Entranced before the door.

Or do I travel as travail of a veil?

This science
Is that séance of the shore, the unsure.

All word-dawn
      is downward, so I raise
Reason to look to lack.

No & no, where the word runs red—
No (cure for suffering): no (furious core).

Because cause
      is curled
In a burning world—
      fact is also
      act, a faked effect.

Call of the best beast, as mind is moaned—

As one commands the other.
      The news comes wrapped
      already ripped.

      (The system of a mystery
Threw this through that.)

THE POVERTY OF FACT

One lizard is less than one word.
Whose tongue unscrolls to taste the dust?

The walls of the mind are painted
Hot pink, the color of electricity.

Either aether or ore, the barrens accumulate.
Forgive me, I have not eaten today.

I am a talking picture, nothing more
Than a tissue wedged between ages of silence.

Frame by frame, the bus window
Animates the still desert.

By the roadside, the skull of Taurus whitens
Beaconwise —

Correspondent to the unspilled sky.
His horns are garlanded with wandering planets.

This evening in the plaza
Heaven is the guitar that plays itself.

Old church, a rubble patch. Stop here to venerate
The bloody stumps of the black cactus.

Canyon I call for no answer.
To be accurate, a man goes back to his ghost.

As the militia guards the volcano, so
Is necessity measured, against the will.

Hecho en México, Mayo 2002

RIFT HABITAT

Why I seem same seam:
    mothered more than once, I
    rail to rule the reel of real.

My sum, some-
    thing
    massed as
    my nothing most mist—

Plangent the plunge, full-throated
    through
My mind-roofed rift.

I invent my inventory in
    inverted time, tangent

    to the sureness of my shore, & its
    voracious shining.

Rending as rendering—

The line, the river
    that has no mouth.

That row that rose: run down, round Sun—

Moon the fullness of
    rune, the form of
    ruin, renewing.

The starry stops, ends
In themselves—

Shape poured empty
    that requires choirs.

The low to console, the high
    to conceal. The call to cancel.

All is all exception—

ATOMS HAVE THEIR HIVE

God, it is to be
      supposed that *Man is in pain.*

Spilt into split, as sigh unto scythe—

Pain is a red scarf
Freed from my body
      & whirled away, a skirl on the wind.

As atoms have their hive
In *have*—
I halve my half forever.

      For: for the maker
      mirrored = marred.

Rhyming *ever over, over ever*

      —quill & quell—

What leaf-turned book, what
     landscape
Read red
     wall of sky, red wall of womb?

A man of sorrows knows no series, so
The sore rose cannot come to sere ease.

Gift of the impossible:
     total fragment that includes only what excludes itself.

     Thus, this
Whisper supports space, as a rumor

     or a room lost within its exact locality.

But a sob neither does nor does not resemble a bell

& wants night & light at once.

TO EACH CORRESPONDENT TO SPEECH

What weight do I await?

I am afraid that
Room is empty, apart from meaning.

Often a cat is trapped in
      all the intricacies of its senses.

—this Paradise
Is a desert
      populated by pillars
      half-human, half-mineral.

      Sun ever sum
Where a term is wanting

      to be called to co-
      ordinates

Horizontal to reason & vertical to vertigo.

I am the house that inhabits me.

As a man is
Unsigned, more than
Mantle
　　　of his mind, there is no master.
The wall, as will, stands still.

Salve me, solve me: my chorus to each
Correspondent to speech.

So no is yet
Yes
　　　& my revealing my reveiling—

LOW LAW

Once flown, own
Fellow fell
     to walk in weak fable.

Followed the flaw in law, took talk

To loot late
Fate, after what interminable weight.

Polis, police, please
     appeal the list of the lost—

A *peal*, a *pull* all-appelative, sole solar apple.
Rotate vote: I over I.

To know the rights of man
& moon.

Anti-echo to call
     one many, & wind mind.

A = A

Mine to ask a mask to say, A is not A.

No one, ever the contrarian, to answer.

The moon is both divided & multiplied
     by water: as chance, as the plural of chant.

O diver, to be sea-surrounded by a thought bled white—
     a blankness as likely as blackness.

What is the word for getting words & forgetting?

Might night right sight?

I, too late to relate
     I & I, trap light in sound
& sing no thing that breath can bring.

ABOUT THE AUTHOR

Born in 1955, Andrew Joron was raised in Stuttgart, Germany, Lowell, MA, and Missoula, MT. He attended the University of California at Berkeley to study with the anarchist philosopher Paul Feyerabend, graduating with a degree in the philosophy of science. After a decade and a half spent writing science-fiction poetry, culminating in his volume *Science Fiction* (1992), Joron turned to a more speculative form of lyric, influenced by German Romanticism and surrealism, and reflecting his association with Philip Lamantia. This later work has been collected in *The Removes* (1999) and in *Fathom* (2003). *The Cry at Zero*, a selection of his prose poems and critical essays, was published by Counterpath Press in 2007 and an expanded version of his study, *Neo-Surrealism; Or, the Sun at Night*, was issued by Kolourmeim Press in 2010. Joron is also the translator, from the German, of the Marxist-Utopian philosopher Ernst Bloch's *Literary Essays* (1998). Joron's latest poetry collection is *The Sound Mirror*, published by Flood Editions. He lives in Berkeley, where he works as a part-time proofreader and indexer. He also plays theremin in the improvisational trio Free Rein.

CITY LIGHTS SPOTLIGHT

1

Norma Cole, *Where Shadows Will:*
Selected Poems 1988-2008

2

Anselm Berrigan, *Free Cell*

3

Andrew Joron, *Trance Archive:*
New and Selected Poems

4

Cedar Sigo, *Stranger in Town*

5

Will Alexander, *Compression & Purity*

6

Micah Ballard, *Waifs and Strays*

7

Julian Talamantez Brolaski, *Advice for Lovers*